Contents

Part One
PS I Love You, Gramps
Pages 2–25

Part Two
Letters Throughout
the Ages
Pages 26–30

Hi, my name is Josie. I live on a small island with my mom and dad, and my sister, Susie, and brother, Tom. My favorite things are rabbits and writing letters. I write lots of letters to my Gramps. He just lives over on the other side of the island, but I still miss him.

Dear Gramps,

Susie and Tom have new sneakers. I did not get any. Soon it will be Pet Day at school. I hope I can take my pet rabbit. Mom's cabbages and tomatoes have little holes all over them. She says they're from the snails and caterpillars.

Love,
Josie

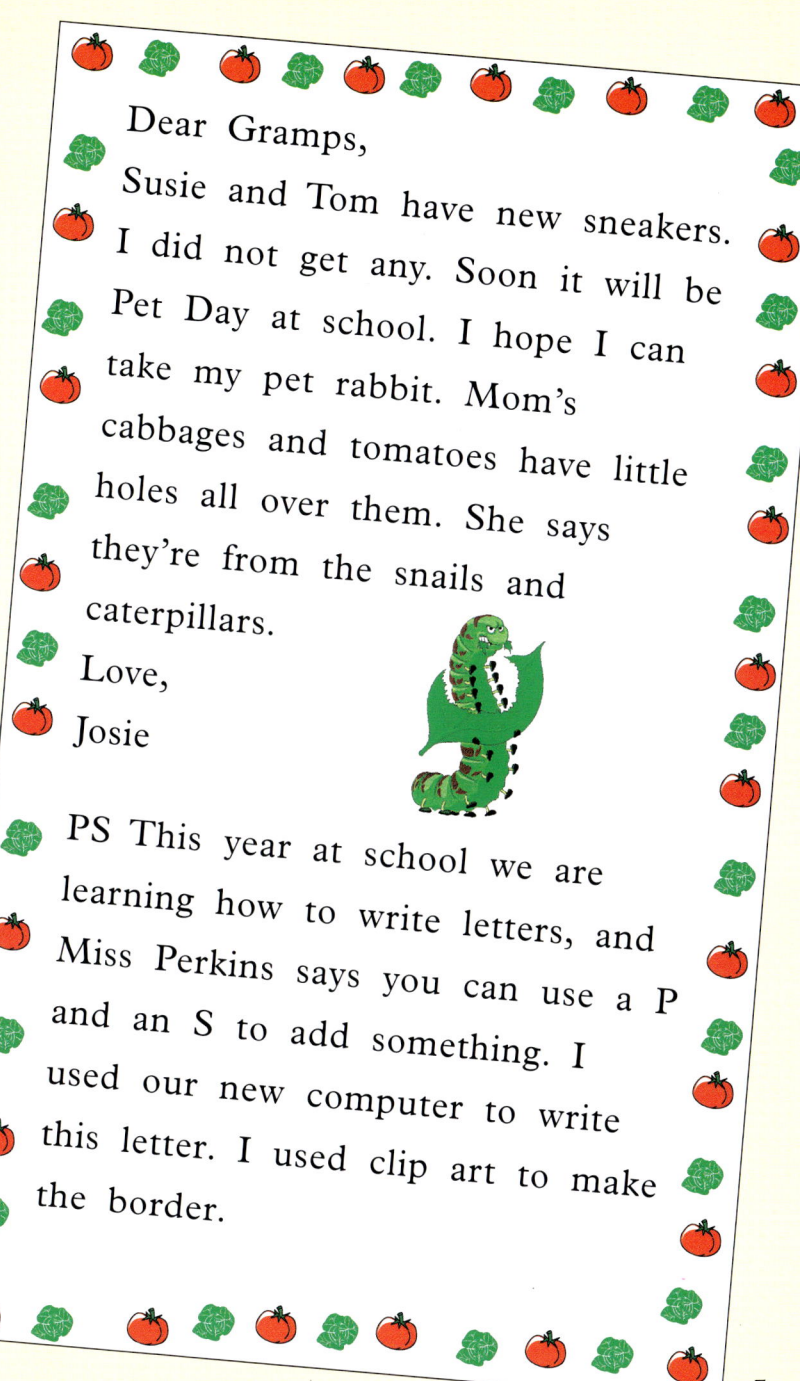

PS This year at school we are learning how to write letters, and Miss Perkins says you can use a P and an S to add something. I used our new computer to write this letter. I used clip art to make the border.

August 23

Dear Gramps,
Mom says she won't buy me new sneakers until I learn how to take better care of things. I left my last pair at Katie's house, and her dog chewed them up. I'm going to call my pet rabbit Flopsy.
The holes in the cabbages and tomatoes are getting bigger and bigger. When are you getting your new fax machine?
Yours sincerely,
Josie

PS Miss Perkins says you should end a letter with "yours sincerely" and you should always put the date. I love you, Gramps.

August 29

Dear Gramps,

    Maybe taking care of sneakers is what you learn in high school. All the kids in my class have sneakers with holes in the toes, like mine.

    No. I have not actually got my rabbit yet, but I think it will have a pretty bow.

    Mom is ~~in des dispar~~ very upset about the cabbages and tomatoes, but they taste alright if you eat around the holes.

Yours sincerely,
Josie

PS Do you like my paragraphs? Miss Perkins says each idea has its own space. Love you.

10 View Road
Half Moon Bay
Conifer Island
September 3

Dear Gramps,

Today it rained and my sneakers got wet. I liked the squelchy feeling, but Mom doesn't like me to have wet socks.

You wanted to know what color my rabbit will be. Well... mostly gray, I think. Mom's pickling cabbage and making tomato relish.

Yours sincerely,
Josie

PS It seems silly to write at the top where I live when you already know, but Miss Perkins says you always do this in letters.

September 12

Dear Gramps,
  It was fun to see your letter come out of the fax. Thank you for being so quick.
  If I get new sneakers, I will get black ones. Black is choice.
  Pet Day is soon. I'll have to get Flopsy quickly so she'll have time to learn her name. Mom says she's making ~~peserv~~ preserves with the holey cabbages and the tomatoes.
  Yours Sincerely,
  Josie
PS Are you coming for Pet Day?

Harold Smithers
Hilltop Farm
Conifer Island

13

10 View Road
Half Moon Bay
Conifer Island
September 18

Dear Gramps,

Today is the best and the worst day of my life. Mom says "Yes" to new sneakers but "No" to a pet rabbit. "What would my garden be like if we had a rabbit as well as snails and caterpillars?" she said.

So, may I please borrow Bonnie for Pet Day? She can give rides.

Yours sincerely,

Josie

PS Do you like my quotation marks? Miss Perkins says they show when someone is talking. Love you.

Miss Josie Smithers
requests the pleasure of the company
of Harold Smithers and Bonnie
at Pet Day to be held
at Half Moon Bay School
on Wednesday, October 11, at 10 A.M.

RSVP October 4
Half Moon Bay School, Conifer Island

10 View Road
Half Moon Bay
Conifer Island
September 30

Dear Gramps,

My class made invitations today to ask you to come to our Pet Day. We hope you can bring Bonnie.

Yours sincerely,

Josie

PS Miss Perkins says we had to send you a formal invitation. The letters "RSVP" stand for "répondez s'il vous plaît," which is French for please reply. That's how we'll know how many cups and saucers to set out. I love you, Gramps.

10 View Road
Half Moon Bay
Conifer Island
October 4

Dear Gramps,

   Wow! Everyone loved the formal reply you sent. It's pinned on the notice board! All the kids are bringing apples for Bonnie's lunch! After school, Mom and I are shopping for my new sneakers and the labels for preserves. Great news!!! Dad's going to show me how to use E-mail on his computer.

Yours sincerely,
Josie

P.S. Miss Perkins says you use exclamation marks to show ~~expresh~~ expression. I love you.

Date: October 9
From: Homebunny@aol.com
To: Htopfarm@aol.com
Subject: New sneakers

Dear Gramps,

Do you like my E-mail code name? Dad says you have to use a code name for E-mail. My new sneakers are great! And Mom's labels look neat. In our classroom, we have thirty-three apples for Bonnie! Miss Perkins said, "Don't bring any more!"

Yours sincerely,
Josie

PS Miss Perkins told me not to overuse exclamation marks, but I really need them today! Love you.

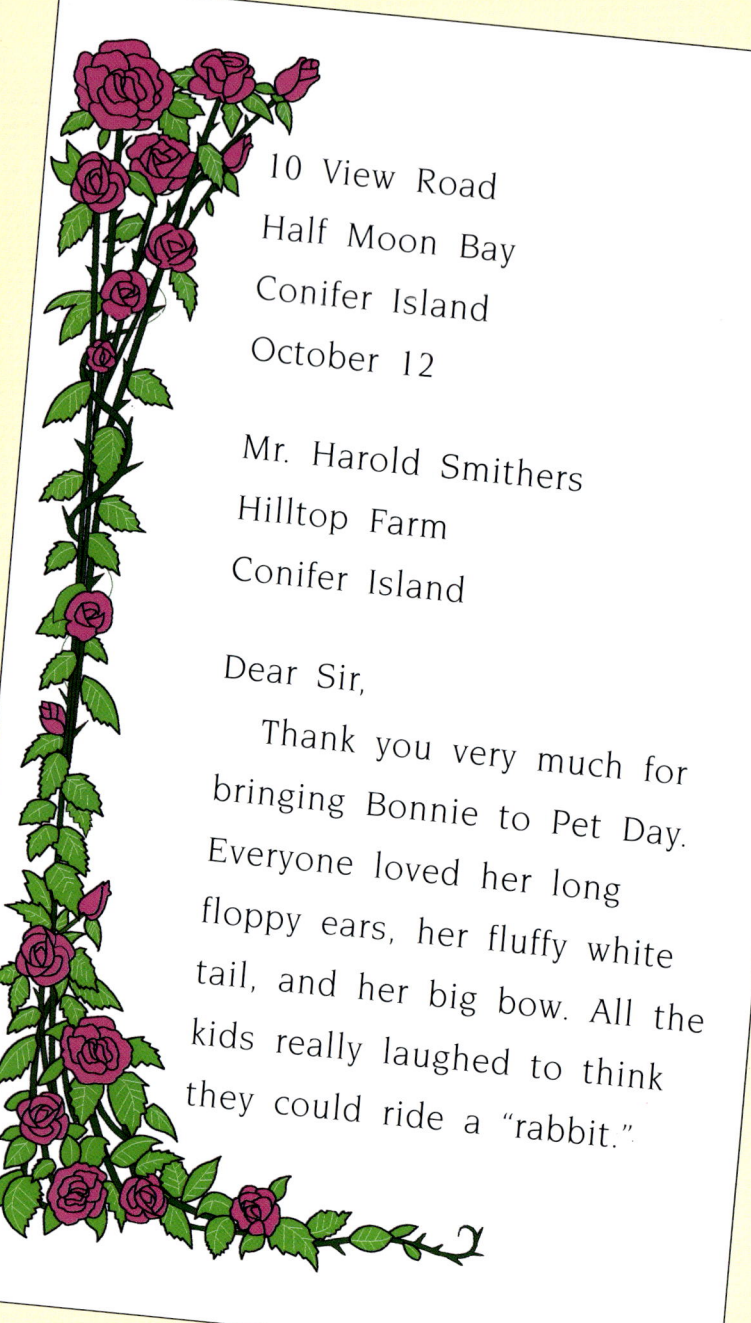

10 View Road
Half Moon Bay
Conifer Island
October 12

Mr. Harold Smithers
Hilltop Farm
Conifer Island

Dear Sir,
    Thank you very much for bringing Bonnie to Pet Day. Everyone loved her long floppy ears, her fluffy white tail, and her big bow. All the kids really laughed to think they could ride a "rabbit."

Does Bonnie keep smiling at her Special Award ribbon? Mom keeps smiling at her Best Tomato Relish ribbon.

I hope you like the jars of pickled "holey cabbage" and tomato relish that she gave you.
Yours faithfully,
Josie

PS Miss Perkins calls this a formal letter. We're writing formal letters to say thank you very politely. But I really want to hug you and shout, "I do love you, Gramps!"

Letters Throughou

Letter writing as a form of communication existed even in ancient times. People learned that written messages were more reliable than spoken ones. A spoken message relied on the messenger having a good memory.

The first letters were delivered by teams of relay runners, who were stationed at points along the major roads. Some letters traveled more than one hundred miles a day!

the Ages

The Romans sent letters by horseback. They built relay stations (called post houses) along the main roads, where a messenger could rest for a while and switch a tired horse for a fresh one.

Above: Letter writers used hot wax to seal their envelopes.

My dear Mamma,
I write my first letter to you, to tell you how dearly I love you, and to wish you many happy re turns of your Birthday. Hoping to see you soon. I am, dear Mamma your dutiful Child
Dora.
Oct 17th/50

Long ago, letters were carefully written in elegant handwriting. Sometimes the writer would decorate letters with pressed flowers, or ribbons, or small watercolor pictures.

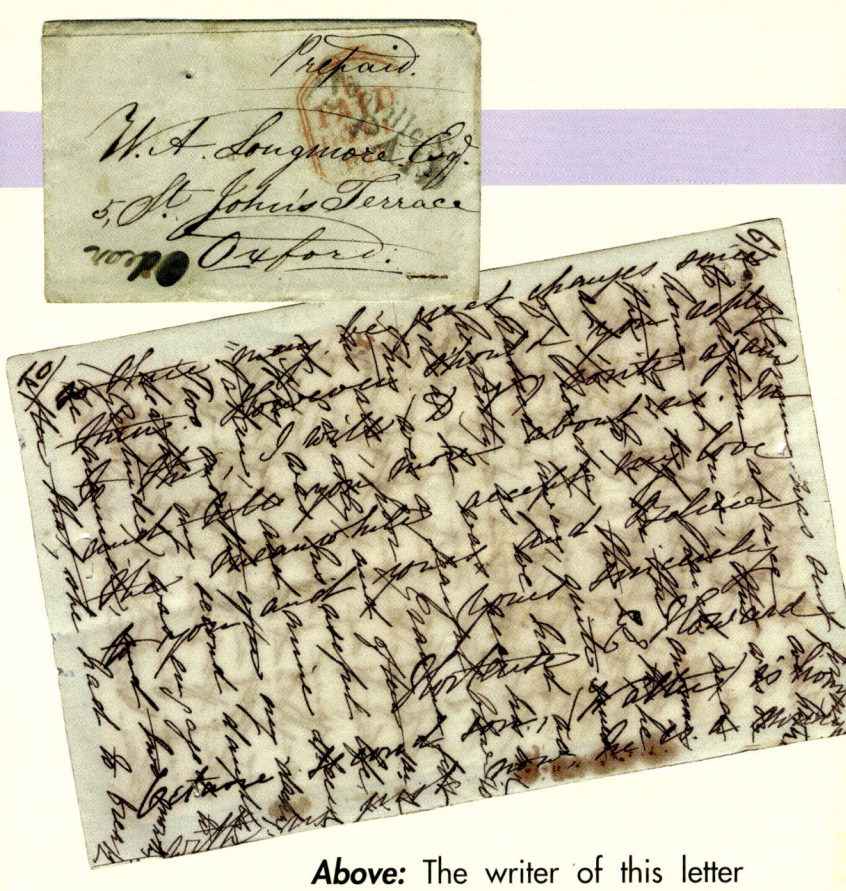

Above: The writer of this letter used every bit of space!

Did you know?

In the past, many people could not read or write. If they wanted to send letters to friends or family they paid a person (called a scribe) to write the letters for them.

Early postcards

Today

Today, letters come in many forms and travel the world in many different ways. Who knows what the letters of the future will be like?

From the Author

I always wanted to write a book, but it was not until I took a summer cruise that the opportunity to write finally came. The "seed," or idea, for my story was sown when my husband and I sailed into a small, offshore island bay, where we visited the local school's Pet Day. As we walked around, admiring the pets, we overheard a parent saying to one little girl, "I like your horse." The little girl replied, "It's not a horse; it's a rabbit!" Her reply surprised us all, and the idea stayed in my memory to spark this story.

Linley Jones

PS The time to "write up my story" came on my long night watches during the cruise home.

FRIENDS AND FRIENDSHIP
Uncle Tease
PS I Love You, Gramps
Friendship in Action
Midnight Rescue
Nightmare
You Can Canoe!

WILD AND WONDERFUL
Winter Survival
Peter the Pumpkin-Eater
Because of Walter
Humphrey
Hairy Little Critters
The Story of Small Fry

ACTION AND ADVENTURE
Dinosaur Girl
Amelia Earhart
Taking to the Air
No Trouble at All!
River Runners
The Midnight Pig

ALL THE WORLD'S A STAGE
All the World's a Stage!
Which Way, Jack?
The Bad Luck of King Fred
Famous Animals
Puppets
The Wish Fish

Written by **Linley Jones**
Illustrated by **Christine Ross** and **Bryan Pollard** (pp. 26-27)
Photographed by **Alan Gillard**
Edited by **Sue Ledington**
Designed by **Kristie Rogers**

© 1997 Shortland Publications Inc.
All rights reserved.

04 03 02 01 00
10 9 8 7 6 5 4 3

Distributed in the United States of America by
    Rigby
    a division of Reed Elsevier Inc.
    P.O. Box 797
    Crystal Lake, IL 60039-0797

Printed by Colorcraft, Hong Kong
ISBN: 0-7901-1644-8